bite size
truth

bite size
truth

meditations for life
book 1

Xin-Rain

BALBOA.
PRESS
A DIVISION OF HAY HOUSE

Balboa Press books may be ordered through booksellers or by contacting:

Balboa Press
A Division of Hay House
1663 Liberty Drive
Bloomington, IN 47403
www.balboapress.com
1-(877) 407-4847

Because of the dynamic nature of the Internet, any web addresses or links contained in
this book may have changed since publication and may no longer be valid. The views
expressed in this work are solely those of the author and do not necessarily reflect the
views of the publisher, and the publisher hereby disclaims any responsibility for them.

The author of this book does not dispense medical advice or prescribe the
use of any technique as a form of treatment for physical, emotional, or medical
problems without the advice of a physician, either directly or indirectly. The
intent of the author is only to offer information of a general nature to help you
in your quest for emotional and spiritual well-being. In the event you use any
of the information in this book for yourself, which is your constitutional right,
the author and the publisher assume no responsibility for your actions.

Any people depicted in stock imagery provided by Thinkstock are models,
and such images are being used for illustrative purposes only.
Certain stock imagery © Thinkstock.

Printed in the United States of America.

ISBN: 978-1-4525-7526-1 (sc)
ISBN: 978-1-4525-7527-8 (e)

Balboa Press rev. date: 07/15/2013

Seeking to draft a foreword or introduction to this work for some time, the author was stumped. The more that was written, the less relevant it appeared to be. Perhaps no preamble was necessary at all.

Reaching out to some fellow authors for advice, a wide range of opinions and approaches were offered. One dear friend shared her thoughts in the form of an invitation. It seemed right. Here it is:

An Invitation

Finding spaciousness . . . the words in this book are all about space . . . white space . . . reflective space . . . breathing space . . . unfettered space. And so, before turning the page, you are invited to create a certain receptive spaciousness within your self by taking a deep breath. Ahhhhhhhhh.

Approach with reverence both the sparseness and depth of words on each page as one would holy ground . . . or a most precious jewel . . . or the vastness of the night sky.

This book is an enigma because it is meant to be anything but a page turner. Rather it is an invitation to simply be . . . still . . . open . . . unhurried . . . present. To be with this book is to abandon the need to get somewhere. Rather you are asked to visit any page as one would sit quietly in the presence of something or someone sacred.

No need to be overly serious either. Rather simply allow the words to roll around in your mouth and tickle your ears. Toss the words in the air and let them land softly on your tongue . . . like snowflakes perhaps . . . melting into your being.

Savor each word, opening your heart and mind to something beyond mere meaning. Seek instead to be awakened or soothed, as the case may be, by their energetic essence. Expect nothing. Surrender to whatever happens . . . knowing that you might visit a page one hundred times and each visit will be a unique experience.

Above and beyond all this, simply delight in the magical serendipity of what can be conveyed in just a few words. And since, if you do, these wisps of wisdom will most assuredly take your breath away. Remember to breathe . . . . Ahhhhhhhhhhhhhhhhhhhhhhhhhh.

*Publisher's Note: This book is designed to be viewed in a two-page spread format, in both digital e-book and printed versions.

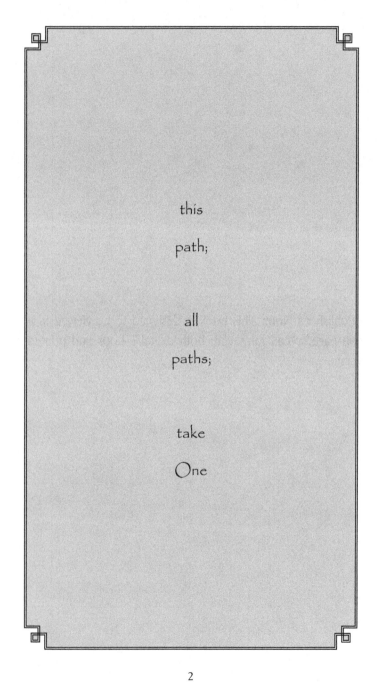

this

path;

all

paths;

take

One

each

name

further

forever

divides

truth

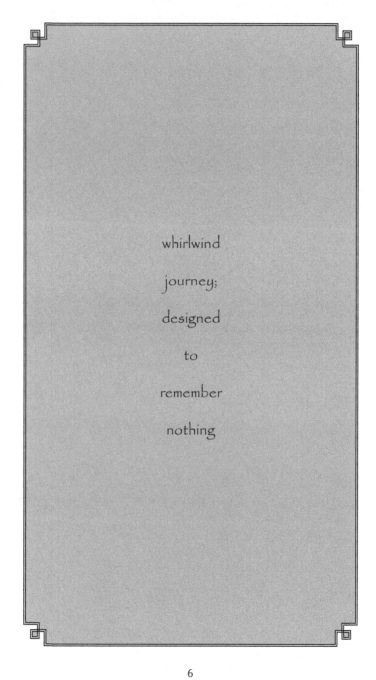

whirlwind

journey;

designed

to

remember

nothing

within

heart's

mind;

mountains

melt

time

truth

reflects

this

page

without

words

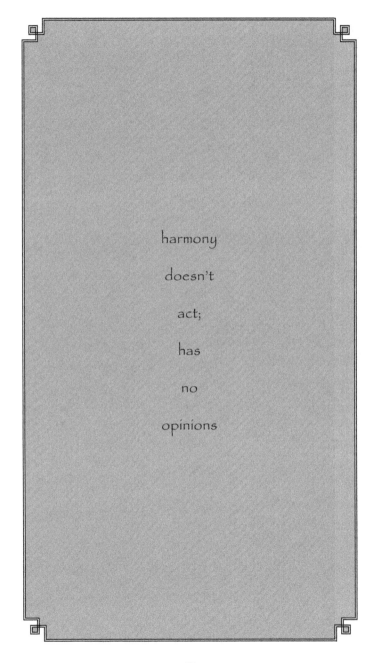

harmony

doesn't

act;

has

no

opinions

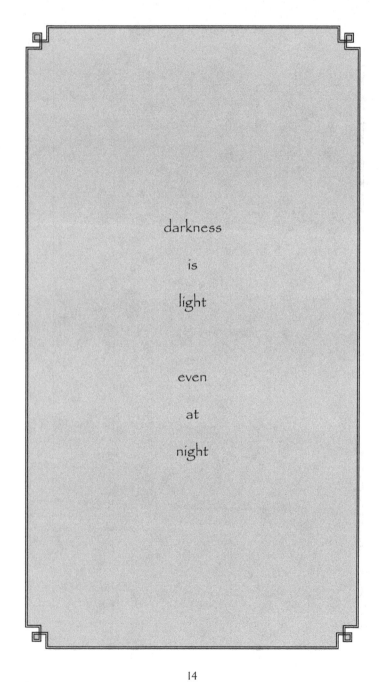

darkness

is

light

even

at

night

now

and

forever

masquerade

as

two

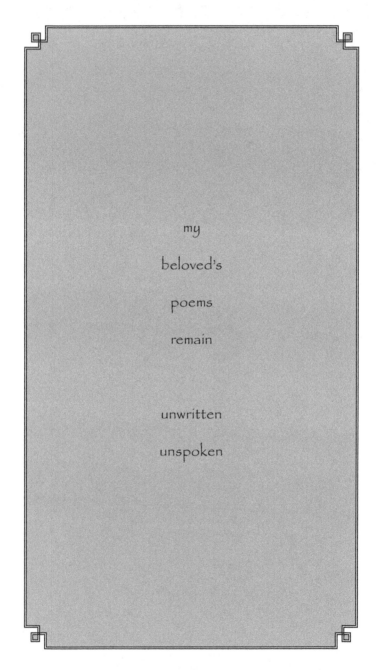

my

beloved's

poems

remain

unwritten

unspoken

through

infinite

eyes

miracles

are

common

this

world's

most

precious

gift;

change

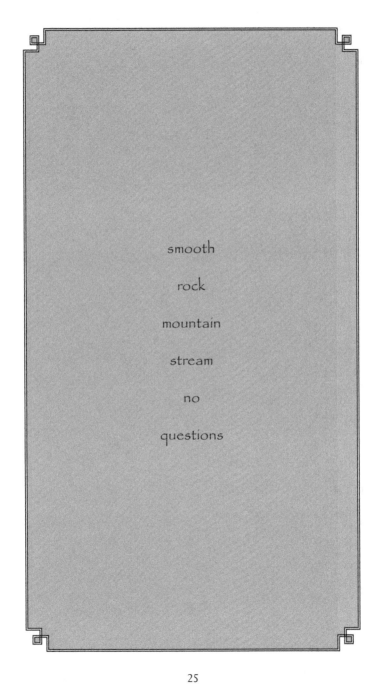

smooth

rock

mountain

stream

no

questions

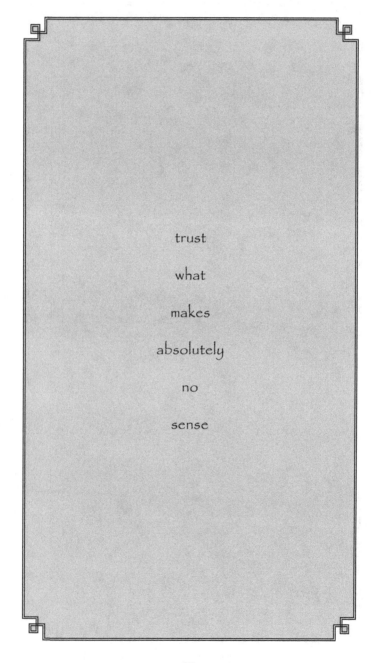

trust

what

makes

absolutely

no

sense

language

ideas

words

distractions

from

light

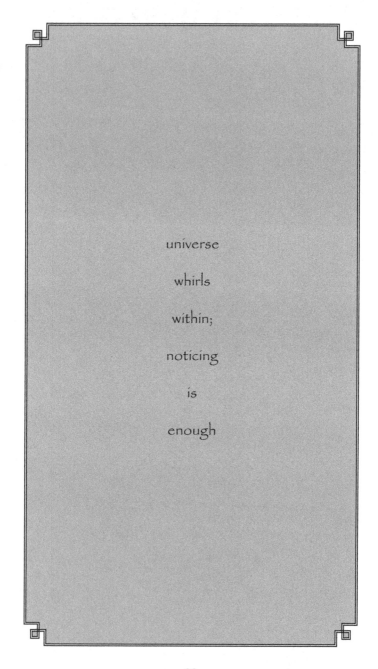

universe

whirls

within;

noticing

is

enough

composition;

the

celestial

kiss;

emptiness

amidst

intention

span;

out

do

your

self

relax;

traction

slips

midday

tea;

sips

dive

deep

within;

awaken

at

splash

your

heart;

this

instant;

shapes

eternity

before

birth;

no

students

no

teachers

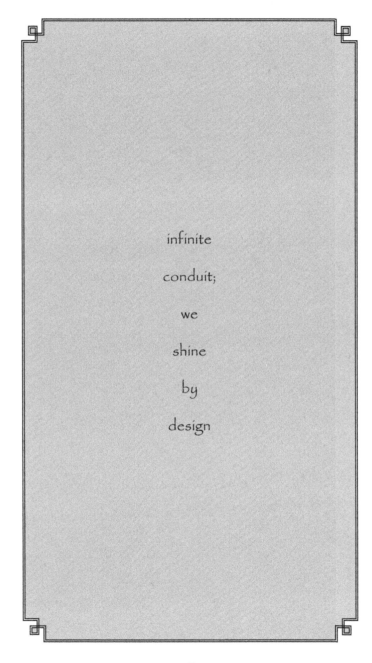

infinite

conduit;

we

shine

by

design

lost

time

in

space;

no

trace

yes

no;

in

constant

flow;

whoa

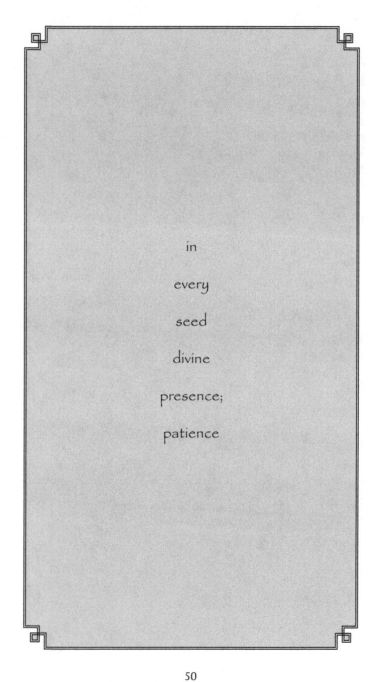

in

every

seed

divine

presence;

patience

remember;

letting

go

requires

no

effort

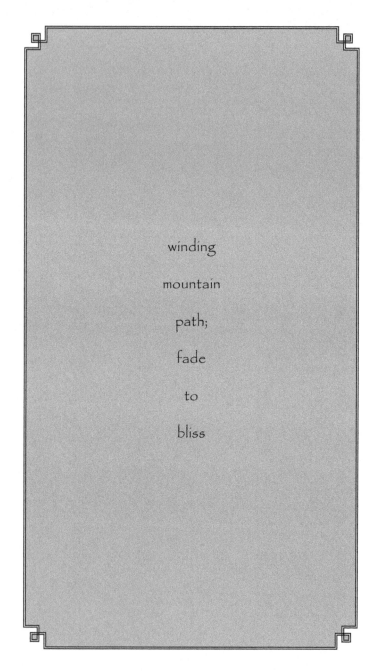

winding

mountain

path;

fade

to

bliss

ancient

dust

wind

tossed;

mind

lost

frosted

pine

needles

soften

with

morning

eternal

bliss

bridge;

each

of

us

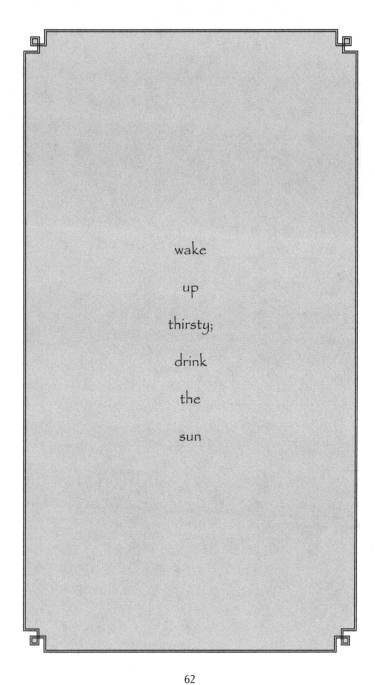

wake

up

thirsty;

drink

the

sun

infinite

abundance

no

sleeves

no

tricks

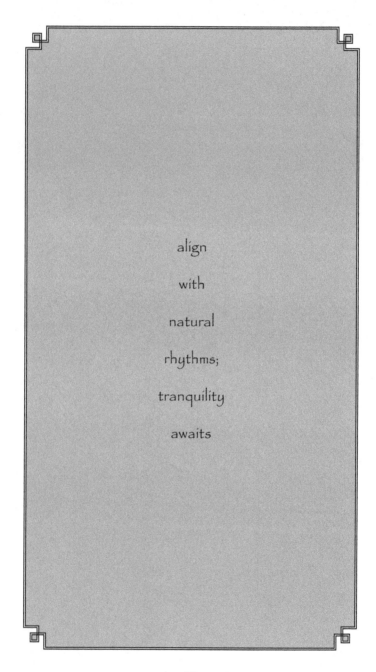

align

with

natural

rhythms;

tranquility

awaits

all

things

happen

before

they

happen

every

thing;

both

dust

and

king

man

made

clock

ticks

don't

exist

end

forgotten

search

finds

itself

beginning

eyelids

close

aspen

shimmers

divine

rewinds

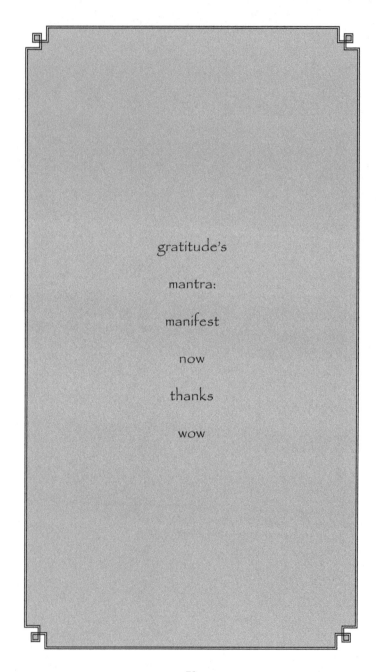

gratitude's

mantra:

manifest

now

thanks

wow

eternity's

ultimate

gift

to

itself;

you

sunset

awakens

sunrise

sleeps

helix

doubles

stay

right

here;

serendipity

finds

you

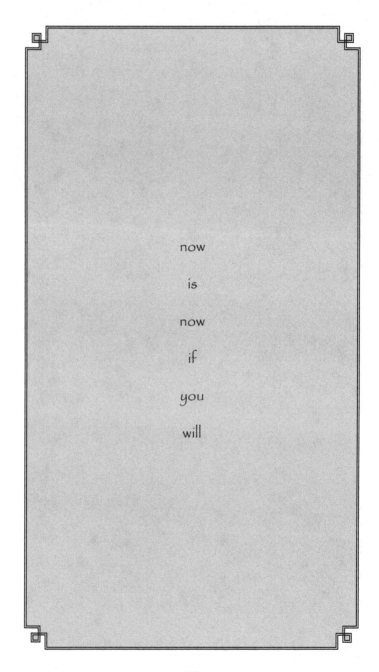

now

is

now

if

you

will

water

shapes

rock;

tao

shapes

us

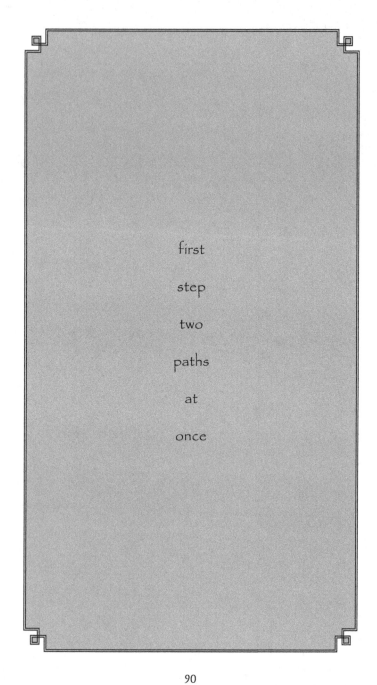

first

step

two

paths

at

once

there

is;

close

your

eyes;

see

what

if;

stillness;

the

preeminent

desire

dreaming

fire

crackling

awake

til

dawn

two

arrows

opposite

directions

bypass

night

notice;

truth

just

can't

shake

simplicity

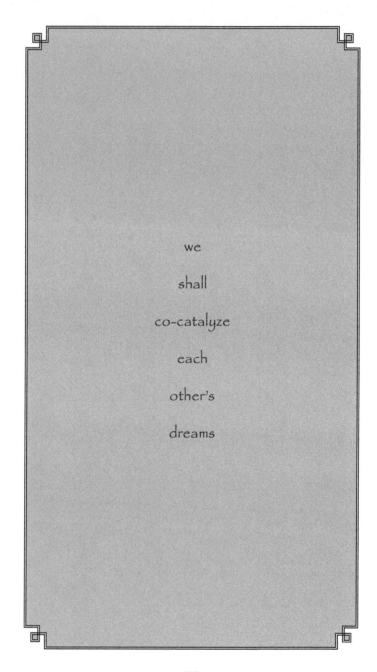

we

shall

co-catalyze

each

other's

dreams

intergalactic

eternal

nectar

taste

of

silence

muddy

water

settles;

patience

naturally

appears

culmination;

eons

at

ease;

bliss

morning

beloved's

remembrance

flowers

eternity;

bees,

rejoice

meditation's

highest

form

remembers

to

forget

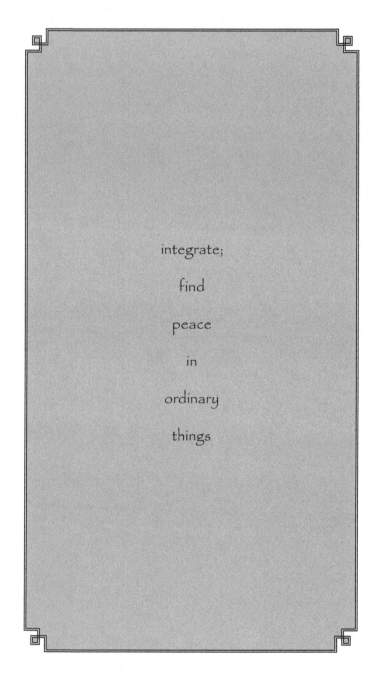

integrate;

find

peace

in

ordinary

things

10,000

monks

eyes

heart

center

wait

love's

intention

manifests

one

collective

heart

they

are

you;

give

em

wings

only

this

breath

unfolds

the

next

what's

inside

without

what's

outside

within

earth

water

metal

fire;

ether

prior

more

isn't

more

more

isn't

more

root

downward

stand

tall

align,

refine

wick

unlit;

we,

as

light;

equipped

steel

grey

cloud

becomes

snow-capped

mountain

ultimate

paradox;

you

are /

not

you

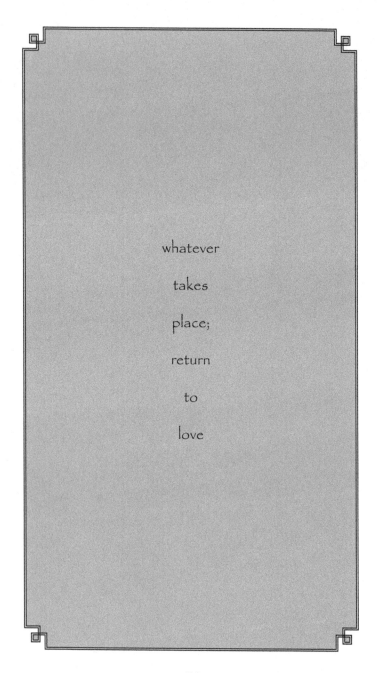

whatever

takes

place;

return

to

love

direct

path

does

not

sidestep

illusion

unaware;

clouds

form,

as

did

you

entendre;

one

then

two

then

through

this

body;

with

without;

i

am

honey

sticks

to

sweetness;

softness

deepens

in

company

of

stars;

you

are

what

seems

most

subtle;

next

gateway

horizon

is

illusion

so

too

illusion

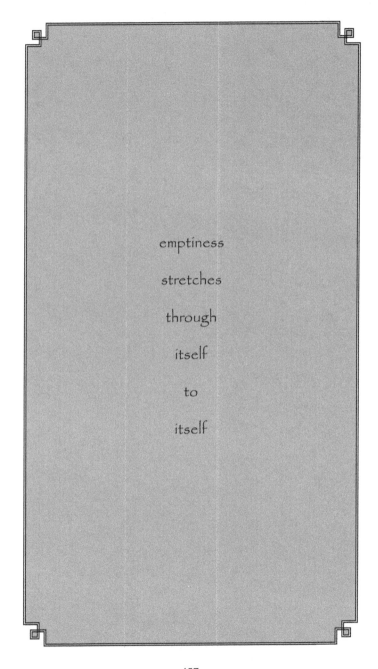

emptiness

stretches

through

itself

to

itself

intention

aligns

first;

fast-forward

is

reverse

thus,

not

knowing

creates

each

miracle

before

words;

much

more

was

said